THE VALLEY OF CRANES

THE VALLEY OF CRANES

PHILLIP FOSS

Singing Horse Press 2010

Singing Horse Press
5251 Quaker Hill Lane
San Diego, CA 92130

Singing Horse Press titles are available directly from the publisher at singinghorsepress.com or from Small Press Distribution (800) 869-7553, or at www.spdbooks.org.

Also by Phillip Foss

Roaring Fork Passage

Grace; The Snakes and the Dogs

House of Eagles

Yana

Somata

The Composition of Glass

The Excesses The Caprices

Courtesan of Seizure

Chromatic Defacement

Venaculture

The Ideation

Imperfect Poverty

CONTENTS

The Valley of Cranes

Zoltan Kodaly: *Sonata for Unaccompanied Violoncello op. 8* [1915]

First Day of a Year Measured in Nights

perhaps in a hundred years I will discover this
and remember · perhaps
I discovered · remembered :

           countenances · each billion un-remembered

like fingers at the loom counting threads ; metaphor
for any mutation desired ;

this is the gesture with which summer's foliage in winter
releases the sky · breathe blue · color lung
since all thing is loss

discarded in every shelter · memorabilia
of each sentience · their detritus
is loved : yucca sandal · silk brasserie

then do I believe in the dearticulation
of any one · in the way that sand
is no longer stone · no longer mountain · not planet

still the clothing worn by earth is only the midden
of its dead · not an idea
recoverable · even in its vocabulary of mandibles · largely

unmeasured · the sea is undermining my continent

this is a natural history :
rain's exact angle is not mechanics but memory
lost trajectories

of desire succoring what soil deems worthy · finger
of hummingbird expatriates like a slogan :
the mummers' paradox is to incorporate
the sky into the mask

so the beginning was a serrated dawn ;
past and imagining folded
like the edge of a paper fan

on which is painted blind men on a log bridge :

this is natural law : reformed forms of oppression

can I assimilate the beauty of women ?

stones are sounds : the voice of breaking
or of the motionless · this juxtaposition
is visual · not acoustic

still · walking through the market · I perceived humanity
as disease · loved most

(each moment I construct · attempt
to reconstruct · as memory)

sad · beautiful
disease ; be thou crystalline geode

(my memory is empty)

in the same way that the sexual eyes
of women are inhuman vocalizations ·

are refracting
stones

this is an indifferent language · a kind of litter
strewing the watercourse where I walk
asleep :   nothing
                 can arrive
                 nothing can depart

                 no thing can be

I wash my hands
of its waters :
        including manifestations of the miraculous :

I am not the cactus eaten in famine
I am not a loon built of star
I am not the moon sipped from the hand

(there is causality for this : the flying raven
                dropping the hare's head in the yard)

abandoned nests ornament leafless trees ;
was I causal in this desecration ?

while I practice the agitation of molecules one raven
strokes past my window lamenting
the infinity of snowflakes :

any such rendering is only phenology tracked
through ideology · as the cry
of the crane falls toward frozen ground

thus not of · but · nature · as a mushroom
pushing up half frozen ground at christmas
yet mushroom is not kingfisher ; still
there can be no difference

: I dreamt this as a landscape flooded with dark water
fore grounded by the seer ricocheting :
billiard ball between white and silver tree trunks

in this I had assumed time was measured vertically

~ ~ ~

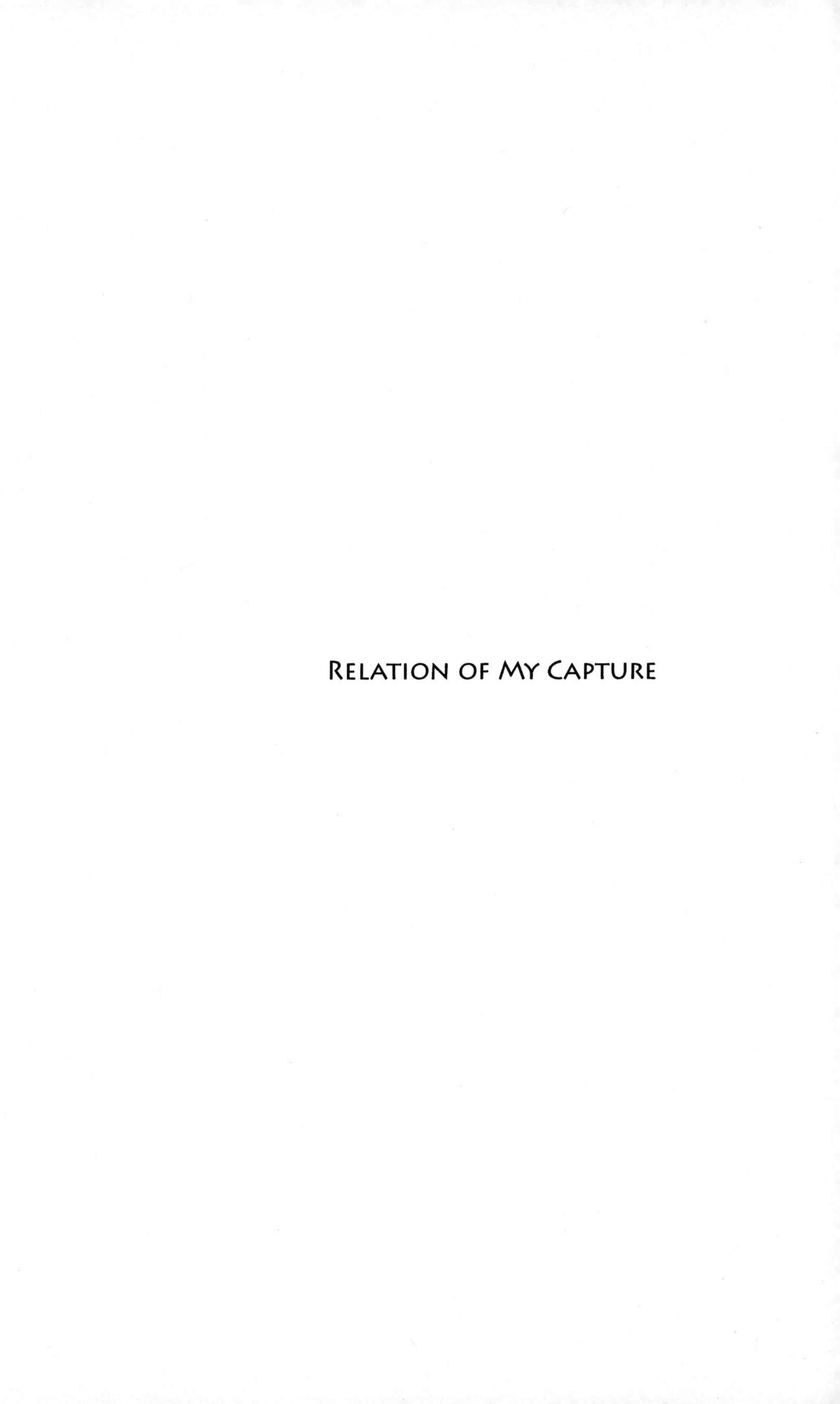

Relation of My Capture

A FOUND WORLD

this is the banquet in heaven : orphan
languishing in eviscerated car seat
abandoned in pine grove

the view :

his ecstatic life streaming
transparent through the forest

documenting where he embarked :
not toward
arrival but retreating from departure

infant · I am walking in an alley loud
with whorled shells of poisoned snails :

they are not a mirror-galaxy ·
but the encroaching
failure of spine
to spin true to orbit :

I abandon the dying :

though fallen · they
are not yet perfect
pine

Agrarian Reform

I am grubbing in the soil ; there is no
food there · not yellow melons
scrimshawed bones yes · forgotten love

perhaps · cartridge casings
green glass shards · mammal
tooth : enough to create
a perfect world

five cranes flow north : only water's errant clouds
their voice is any · as river is a ribbon of sky

seen from sky

I sleep dreaming of mushrooms
or brains seeping
up out of the earth

the wind is brutal today ; I can smell kyoto
at least the odor of a dropped rice grain in a pantry ;
smell the breath of the man malleting the bell

(always the iron odor of the bell's sound)

the cranes are silent · fixated on tundra

a world larger than mine ;
I examine the soil again for shallots
or mollusks :

only shells for fleshing hides · hides for clothing
the nakedness of the moon

perhaps I was awakened here and realized
lunar influence on water
perhaps I confused moon with crane :

my body having no water

Ladder to First Cave

For Vaughn & Marcia

too cold to melt this old
snow · even the air is silent

in splitting · the frozen firewood shouts ·
lake ice breaking

nuthatch scurries head down down
bark imitating flakes' fall

someone walking breaking roof's
ice crust : horned owl

masonry-faced cliff dwellings · pissing
into their abandoned snow stream

no maize here · even colonial
apple gone wild : cholla

soot-blackened caves · how many
meals ? smoky laughter ?

beautiful women smelling
of smoke aggregate any future

splash ale-hops on ice-buried
garlic : next autumn's meals

trumpeter pigeon stomping ·
trumpeting · making weak sun rise

ice storm shatters trees · as fuel
next winter's foil to that ice

almond trees naked · scrub
jay tries to remember

high wind · trees in semaphore :
language I don't know

juniper fire popping : old
ones rhythmically dying

head lights creeping across
mountain · no roads

snow inundating my valley · I feel cold :
every window open

winter so bitter
I burn the heart
to warm four beans

GLASS

birds die
against the window escaping
hawks · believing in transparency ·
in the ability of light
to translate form

I've tired of mortality ·
the shucking
of bodies · the dressing
of faces

digging

the largest moon
of the year
staggers my shadow · every body
above me has died · the moon

blows a white wind : ospreys ·
choreographed souls ·
define glass

THE KREAUTZER SONATA

there are gestures to catch
mind falling :

this damned willow keeps sighing ;
keeps being

can sound · bereft of signifier ·
mean

he counted his coffee beans · not his stars ;

rufus towhee scatters
red leaves looking ; it is
dancing on a chromatic mirror · no death

great universal stirring

I dreamed he used tweezers
to pluck his anvil and pistil ;
deafened to the crescendos

 he only imagined

the sound from the plucked
violin string is glass

(this whispering · always the gossip
 or singing · I cannot define)

the dancer is blind · cannot
read music · cannot be deaf
and still be slave

I watched the alluvial hillside
collapse
and its vicious sound
was benign :

endless flesh-clothed bones
happily alive ;

or sunlight

the issue is petrified hearing · as I hear
bellowing at night

fighter planes dividing cloud

or

this morning the mountains were gone ;
divine misunderstanding · why

the bottoms of women's feet
and the winter's early nightfall
make me incoherent :

then no meaning in any thing · any note ·
sound ? no measure
to any thing ; lifespan folded :

glued origami

this pecked writing in stone
is tedious ;
the glyphic gods · warnings ·
jokes
require an audience

not to hear · understand · is mute ·
yet evocative of an uttered name

probably in another language ·
or alphabet

say the glyph for water
defaced by light
from stone

as in hearing

I suppose name it · sad ·
that sonata is reduced to chemistry :
applaud phosphorous · death lord ·
and nitrogen

the last grain of wheat in the granary ·
mother of ten thousand

sonatas

or births · I suppose ·
as quantifiable : loess

still · the small pile of compost
which is my body is blue light · my goal ·

as can too hope

is this about sacrality of sound ? raven
ghosting "walk walk" while I follow
whistles into a black canyon

or perhaps the flautist in the red dress
is already red
stone · vibrating loss

staccato sleet falling on red roof ?

yes · I believe
cirrus is sound

illiterate to notation · what
signs sound ? hears sound
as symbol · can speech
as sound represent sound
as sound ?

perhaps he evolved
temporally · laterally ·
juxtaposing his living
against dying · as verbs

it being deception ;

then name it sympathetic
resonance · as in ·
impassive
strings

in reducing music to sound one
confuses mountain with sand ·
song is not word · although carp
is water

still ·

these notes are only arranged
sound : woven
pine needles · astronomically placed
stones · imagined
zodiacs ; nothing

still

there is no way to speak
musical notation ; the inscription ·

no language
is ice bird ;

defines nothing ;
is sun dog ;

categorizes nothing ;
flowing glass ;

is nothing articulated :

rooster crane struts after hen ;
a glimpse of swamp ·
bordering rushes ; pine sunset
is the audition of any red

~ ~ ~

THE CRANES

what is the world's architecture ? : centipede
as gesture ; carp mutating into ram ; gypsy
moth to hummingbird ?

I am watching trees blossom ·
in memory · but the past is echoic :
the piano reverberating through

the forest is only time misplaced ·
the player's hands bleeding
into transparency · reverting to glass

as any clothing woven by hand disarticulates ·
its blue borders gone fugitive into sky ·
its white diamonds : mute snow

so too the edifices of culture :
watching the beatitudes of its longing
spray out as mere ceramic scatter

yet between shards of pottery and fingernails
I am incapable of deciphering ; between incisors
and speech ; between migratory flight

and my · or any · memory

the preferred pigments are black
on white · or · in inversion · gnostic rents
of light through the astral dome

still · this is where the chatter
of thought becomes chromatic ·
becomes visual dissonance :

(I want hematite on kaolin : this *is* meaning)

meaning that the emotive skin
of hues are exiled and the narrative
of line is ascendant :

not piano keys · not their dualism ·
no · not fracture · no
merely mud

the mud relented
and let the birds ascend ; birds
modeled of mud · into blue air

in spring · tens of thousands
flying north · escaped souls
impersonating cranes

(they sing ·
 but I cannot read music)

on tundra · in fog · I see them
as viscous ghosts beckoning
toward some insatiable departure :

bichromatic pictograph
painted on pottery
pushed into a dead man's face

giving him directions
for fugitive flight

you see this light coming from the top
of my head ?

it is a speech pattern · my stuttering ·
a way of describing
the relation of shadow to light ·
inhalation to exhalation

describing the way birds' wings move air ·
projecting their voices
toward some benevolent heaven

describing the way · by rain or wind · shards ·
gesturing in design ·
are scattered indiscriminately

the way cannot be reassembled
nor rediscovered
any soul flight

the world is confirmed in centipede ·
in gypsy moth ·
by asphyxiated fingers

there is the replication of piano
music in aspens ·
but there is no hearer

there remains the memory
of ceramics depicting the certitude
of our longing

still · the cranes
circle confused
above two diverging rivers :

they are seeking
their coordinates from the north
star · magnetic field ·

the aurora borealis ;
but they are receiving
directives from black

glyphs dancing across
pots punctured
over their near singing faces

~ ~ ~

THE VULGAR LANGUAGES

Votive Boat

fallen spruce needles
are coated with white ash :
perhaps my burnt bones or the memory
of exploded stars

my knees are bloodied · this crawling
in search of trilobite
or meteorite

yet I hear no voice recounting
past lives · evocations
of deed-based accountability ·
like being born blind
for seeing

if I shuffle under this sandstone
cliff long enough I will find perfect
arrowheads or my perfect
alignment with the planet

will find every lost face
mimicked in the floor's dust

not snow · this rain of tree seed ·
only seminal fluid to dirt

for yang wan-li (1127-1206)

I've tended this patch of dirt
for thirty years : herded ants · pollinated
flowers · seeded clouds

lying on my back the magnetic field
hums through my spine ; horsetail
cirrus are embedded in my irises

and though the tree's shadow is freezing
my left arm · the sun
is burning my right

this spring's pollen fog
is growing in my armpits ·
yeasts are blossoming in my bowels

but I'm confused who this is ·
how he is merely this same dirt
I plant with leeks

in answer I light the juniper wood
fire · freeing the milky way
to finally bloom

burning brown dog · brown sage stick
stick chronograph in wind

small wedge of orange light ·
in this meaning · I see parity

who flies down from the valley
of cranes intact ?

ravens · fiercely coiffured
chanting : *walk* · *walk*

every animal hears this differently
defers to · I found a brain

among the stream cobbles
vortices bright with pyrites

~ ~ ~

THAT THE MOUNTAIN WALKS IS FOOL'S MAGIC; THAT I WALK IS MIRACULOUS

first I was a fist-sized stone of granite
then as a human I flew into jumbled black mountains

second I was a young woman
who had lost her luggage in yellow light

or the illegal immigrant next door
whistling like a mocking bird

then she said the blossoms of the spanish broom
smell like an old woman in a vegetable market

and that in the making of micaceous bowls
the soul is not screened from the clay

as a man I wonder about my sexuality as a woman
wonder about the effect of yellow light
on my eyes

as a cricket I know I can become the woman
and say bright things like
" sun "

TRASH

the child in the road is not

a wind-blown bag

of blood and bone

nor the offering of an owl's call

while the woman dying from breeding

marrow is no longer

mimicking bach's cadences

but hallucinating my imagined

performance of last

rites

and hearing sobbing I examine the pine

casket's exquisite

knots

register a woman's muscular

calves

hear the ancient irrigation

ditch repeat its proven litany

see a tanager flash yellow

flash orange

and watch the aged assume the face

they wore before

any birth

The Gestures of Insects

I am burning my past · one remembered voice
to each flame · one breath to each ashen
memory

these faces flare up · gestures flutter to leaves
goodbye goodbye

I am as much the budding elm
as ice-bent light : cloud reflected in junco's eye
is residue of my history

succulents are rising · this is meaning
that sun is rising · only relation

cranes rattling sky is fracture of winter
I place ear to ground
hear only blood hissing

flocks of birds attack my house :
how do I gauge my value
to a disfigured world ?

I name what I foresee : the past ; my future
is what I imagined

as a body ; I have assembled
a display of memorabilia from my past
which I do not recognize

geese seemingly follow contrails · juniper smoke
scent sinks · war in every animal expression

comprise a moment are · in fact · mirrorings
of each other · perhaps merely synonyms
eviscerated ideas

the storm died · lies in the valley ; clouds
of pink blossoms fall ; war planes grate across
the floor of heaven

the fragile bit of web · thumb to finger · is metaphor
for my still-standing ; the stare

of the hummingbird yields no accessible reading
yet fragile idea : any light · these designs · conspire

to

Natural Law

because the stone house
moves · we worship ground

or wind blowing through bare trees
is unopposed · imperialist · with no
intent

then it is indifference · not
failure · that casts
any life : white blossoms
on the black branch
are frozen rain

or the cicada is encased in clear ice

or the voluptuous
spring storm : blue mountains
obscured by the dust
of a million human bodies

or being no one · not two
I find myself vegetal · dead wood

forgive my non differentiation
the sun caused this

or embers fading · disassembled dream :

wild quail eating cooked
rice ; flicker digging ants ;
larva burrowing tongue :

to cause the least suffering

we strive · starve
no worship · all worship

or one petal veers violet

VERTICAL ROAD TO THE DESCENDING NORTH

no town further than this ; not even wind
reaches here · spruce-canopied trail
is named road · always swivels north · even as south
always sidles west · even as east
never existed

there are no people here · they hold no language

there is no day here · my sole day was tomorrow

examining a raven's skull
on the forest floor
I learn nothing of blackness

only architecture

willing is always memory · the venerable grandmother
bending to lift
a cup of stream
is merely an aspen

I came here to begin life · leaving
I deceive my inception

there is a green frog floating on a downstream
leaf · there is a horned moon in my cup

before I was born
notables spoke
after I was born
they had putrefied

no provenance of wind · or kite
of feather · film or idea · no believing

in any flight or falling · never raptor appetite
no never lust for oblique air

I left before dawn in a moonless night
and the narrow track devolved
into a valley where villagers
had stoked their hearths bright
creating the illusion that starscape
and landscape were seamless

fire in any fallacy
one merely closes eyes
abrogates memory

and any road walks cleanly
into some proclaimed milky way

then notice that something as simple as the sun
here is · in existing
dependant on belief

there was no sun that night no
moon each night the village
dogs yawn at the absolute
end of no spectrum

at dawn I fell through a rainbow

in picking pine nuts from the forest floor
jays claim world

which is light

sitting by the taut barbed wire
I confuse its vibration with women singing

behind me

in ravine-huddling junipers
a church bell calls to worship

the road is strewn with migrating crows beak-plucking
each flowering
flake of snow · in these

I have the distinct sensation
of merely receding

~ ~ ~

Phillip Foss is the author of twelve pervious books and chapbooks of poetry, most recently *The Ideation* and *Imperfect Poverty*, both from Singing Horse Press. Additionally, he has received the Fund for Poetry Award and two Poetry Fellowships from the National Endowment for the Arts. He was founding director of the Creative Writing Program at the Institute of American Indian Arts and editor of *Tyuonyi* magazine. He lives with his wife, Joyce, in northern New Mexico.

Singing Horse Press Titles

Charles Alexander, *Near Or Random Acts.* 2004, $15.00
David Antin, *John Cage Uncaged Is Still Cagey.* 2005, $15.00
Rae Armantrout, *Collected Prose.* 2007, $17.00
Julia Blumenreich, *Meeting Tessie.* 1994, $6.00
Linh Dinh, *Drunkard Boxing.* 1998, $6.00
Norman Fischer, *Success.* 1999, $14.00
Norman Fischer, *I Was Blown Back.* 2005, $15.00
Norman Fischer, *Questions/Places/Voices/Seasons.* 2009, $16
Phillip Foss, *The Ideation.* 2004, $15.00
Phillip Foss, *Imperfect Poverty.* 2006, $15.00
Phillip Foss, *The Valley of Cranes.* 2010, $15.00
Eli Goldblatt, *Without a Trace.* 2001, $12.50
Mary Rising Higgins, *)cliff TIDES((.* 2005, $15.00
Mary Rising Higgins, *)joule TIDES((.* 2007, $15.00
Lindsay Hill, *Contango.* 2006, $14.00
Karen Kelley, *Her Angel.* 1992, $7.50
Karen Kelley, *Mysterious Peripheries.* 2006, $15.00
Kevin Killian & Leslie Scalapino, *Stone Marmalade.* 1996, $9.50
Hank Lazer, *The New Spirit.* 2005, $14.00
McCreary, Chris & Jenn, *The Effacements / a doctrine of signatures.*
    2002, $12.50
David Miller, *The Waters of Marah.* 2002, $12.50
Andrew Mossin, *The Epochal Body.* 2004, $15.00
Andrew Mossin, *The Veil.* 2008, $15.00
Paul Naylor, *Playing Well With Others.* 2004, $15.00
Gil Ott, *Pact.* 2002, $14.00
Ed Roberson, *The New Wing of the Labyrinth.* 2009, $15
Ted Pearson, *Encryptions.* 2007. $15.00
Susan M. Schultz, *Dementia Blog.* 2008, $15.00
Heather Thomas, *Practicing Amnesia.* 2000, $12.50
Rosmarie Waldrop, *Split Infinities.* 1998, $14.00
Lewis Warsh, *Touch of the Whip.* 2001, $14.00

These titles are available online at **www.singinghorsepress.com**,
or through Small Press Distribution, at (800) 869-7553, or online at
www.spdbooks.org.